NOW WHAT?

America's Top Criminal Lawyers Reveal Their #1 Tips
for Families Facing a Legal Crisis

Seven Falls Publishing

NOW WHAT?

America's Top Criminal Lawyers Reveal Their #1 Tips
for Families Facing a Legal Crisis

Andrew R. Curry

The publisher of this book is generously donating all royalties from the retail sales of "**NOW WHAT?**" to:

St. Jude Children's Research Hospital

The mission of St. Jude Children's Research Hospital is to advance cures, and means of prevention, for pediatric catastrophic diseases through research and treatment. Consistent with the vision of founder Danny Thomas, no child is denied treatment based on race, religion or a family's ability to pay.

You can learn more about
St. Jude Children's Research Hospital by visiting
www.stjude.org

This book was made possible by tips from the following:

The Law Offices of John D. Rogers

Julia Jayne, Jayne Law Group

The Law Offices of Saul Bienenfeld, P.C.

Thomas Daly, Criminal Defense Attorney

Phillip Moffit, Attorney at Law

Roger P. Foley, The Law Office of Roger P. Foley

Michael J. Palumbo, Palumbo & Associates P.C.

The Law Office of Edward J. Blum

The Law Offices of Gerald E. Smith

Maureen F. Baldwin-Domes, Attorney At Law

Daniel Izquierdo, Criminal Defense Attorney in Miami, FL

Tigran Martinian, Martinian & Associates, Inc.

Guiseppe Rosselli, Attorney at Law

Howard Greenberg, Attorney at Law

Labe M. Richman, Attorney at Law

Jeff Davis, NYC Criminal Defense Lawyer

Gregg A. Pinto, Attorney at Law

Mahmoud R. Rabah, Attorney at Law

Joseph Indusi, Attorney at Law

Jeff Weiner, Former President of National Association of Criminal Defense Lawyers, based in Miami, FL (NACDL)

Shannon B. Schott, Esq.

David Storobin, Attorney at Law

The Law Offices of Robert Osuna, P.C.

Erik B. Jensen Attorney At Law

Antonio G. Jimenez, Attorney at Law

Robert L.S. Angres, Esq.

S. Michael Musa, Criminal Defense Attorney New York

Kleon C. Andreadis, Attorney at Law

Joshua Adams, Attorney at Law

The Appellate Law Office of Stephen N. Preziosi

Paul Neuharth Jr., APC

Bijan Sebastian Parwaresch, Former Prosecutor

SIXTH AMENDMENT TO THE UNITED STATES CONSTITUTION

In all criminal prosecutions, the accused shall enjoy the right to a speedy and public trial, by an impartial jury of the State and district wherein the crime shall have been committed, which district shall have been previously ascertained by law, and to be informed of the nature and cause of the accusation; to be confronted with the witnesses against him; to have compulsory process for obtaining witnesses in his favor, and to have the Assistance of Counsel for his defence.

CONTENTS

FOREWORD

The unexpected news that a loved one has been arrested for a crime can create a tremendous amount of anxiety for the friends and family of the accused.

The hours and days following an arrest can be filled with the panic, fear and uncertainty around the process and important decisions that need to be made... decisions that should only be made with the consultation of knowledgeable attorney.

The goal of this book is to provide some relief and insight into these processes and decisions.

The information contained in these pages is not to be construed as legal advice in any way. Legal advice should be tailored to the specific circumstances and facts of each situation. Consult an attorney before taking any action based on information contained here.

It's important to understand that the information in this book comes from attorneys all over the country. The laws and procedures may differ from state to state and will not always be applicable to every jurisdiction.

CHAPTER ONE

THE BIG TAKE AWAY – WHAT EVERY READER MUST KNOW

As I was half way through accumulating the necessary information for this unique book, some things became glaringly obvious. I had to make sure that you, dear reader, knew these things.

What I'm going to reveal are things that attorneys may chuckle about because it is so basic to them. Yet, every attorney that mentioned it had numerous clients who often sabotaged their own cases.

What am I talking about?

Miranda Rights!

Here are your Miranda Rights:

☐ You have the right to remain silent.

☐ Anything you say can and will be used against you in a court of law.

☐ You have the right to an attorney.

☐ If you cannot afford an attorney, one will be appointed for you.

<u>That said, the most important advice a criminal attorney will tell you is this:</u>

Do <u>NOT</u> Talk!

In case you're not sure what I mean, let me restate it a different way:

Shut Up!
Remain Silent!
Say Nothing!
Zip It!

What does this mean? If you're arrested, regardless of guilt or innocence, SAY NOTHING!!!!

The only exception, " I want my lawyer". Other than that, say nothing.

Nada!

As you read through the tips we put together for you, it will become obvious how important this suggestion is. One thing stood out for me about this was that innocent folks could be found guilty by just accidentally remembering something a little differently when recalled. Or, even an innocent bystander arrested for probable cause could be charged with the crime just for saying they were at the place where the crime occurred. Again… say NOTHING to the police.

Police are trained to get information out of you – and they will if you don't keep quiet.

The second most glaring thing that stood out from these interviews is this:

Be very polite and easy to get along with.

Although I inherently understood why, I asked an attorney to explain why. Basically, acting like a jerk makes you come across as guilty of the crime. In other words, if you're arrested for a drug crime and you act like an ass, that seems to validate you did the crime.

Yet, if you're arrested for a drug crime and you come across as polite, nice, etc., it doesn't seem to validate you did the crime. The idea comes across as: This is a nice, friendly person, and they don't seem like they would do this crime. It helps create a question in the mind of whether or not you did it. (Excluding things like overwhelming evidence that you committed the crime)

The third and most glaring tip you should remember is this.

When you're arrested and/or charged with something, do NOT take it lightly. Come out swinging with all you have.

This became apparent when I interviewed an attorney about murder. He stated how shocked he was to see those who were charged with murder take it so nonchalantly. He intimated how serious the charge is yet people very often act like they were just picked up for shoplifting a pack of gum and they shrug their shoulders and say, "My lawyer will take care of it."

His advice? **Come out swinging!** Get a lawyer with the experience in the field you need and make sure he can do the job!

The analogy is like this. If you were having heart trouble, would you go to a general M.D. and have him operate on you? Of course not! Your life is on the line (just as it is legally) and you would INSIST on someone who has had the experience, schooling, and patients who are alive and well to validate that doctor is the one you want.

One last thing.

This book was put together by asking top attorneys what their #1 tip is for the crime for which someone is arrested. For example, we asked attorneys this. "What is your #1 tip for someone who was arrested for a drug crime?"

Their response follows under each chapter according to the crime someone was arrested for.

CHAPTER TWO

WHAT IF SOMEONE IS ARRESTED FOR ASSAULT?

Tip from the Law Offices of John D. Rogers

The number one thing that any individual arrested for any crime should do is remain silent. One of the most damaging pieces of evidence that the prosecutor uses against someone in court is their own statement made to police officers.

The next piece of advice for someone arrested for assault with a deadly weapon is to contact an attorney as soon as possible. Generally, people make the mistake of getting bailed out immediately and waiting to contact an attorney until a week before their court date. The problem is that sometimes there are valuable pieces of evidence out there such as video recordings from businesses, footage of the incident captured on mobile devices, or additional witnesses that the police never contacted.

Obtaining an attorney at the earliest possible juncture is beneficial because witnesses' memories tend to fade. By contacting an attorney early, the attorney will contact those witnesses, get a statement, and look for any outstanding video footage that might exist. This is crucial because the longer one waits, the easier it is for critical pieces of evidence to be lost, destroyed, or rerecorded, and for key memories of the incident to fade.

Sometimes cases of assault with a deadly weapon can be a misunderstanding. What an attorney can do is contact the prosecuting agency early after their arrest, and before they are formally charged by the prosecutor's office. Contact them and submit something called a mitigation package; character letters, certificates, etc., that says, "Hey, this client could be charged as a felony or it could be charged as a misdemeanor. This is my client's first offense. He or she is a very good person and comes from a respectable family. Charge this person with a misdemeanor, let's avoid a felony." Usually the mitigation package is fairly successful, but the longer one waits to take that action, the higher chance that the prosecutor will charge them with a felony. Early intervention by an attorney could reduce someone's exposure significantly. A misdemeanor carries one year in a county jail, whereas assault with a deadly weapon is a felony with a two to four years sentence in state prison.

Don't make a statement. Contact an attorney at the earliest possible time to get started, preserve evidence, and perhaps contact the prosecuting agency in order to limit the client's exposure.

In the event that you have a public defender, you don't get assigned a public defender until your first day in court; that could be six weeks, but if you obtain a private attorney it's instantaneous, they're with you, and they can immediately get started on the case.

Tip from Julia Jayne, Jayne Law Group

I would say 75-80% of people arrested for domestic violence are never charged. It's probably the biggest number of arrests that don't lead to charges. Sometimes individuals are arrested for assault with a deadly weapon and not charged because there's not enough evidence.

If someone's arrested for assault with a deadly weapon, frankly, it's really no different than any other arrest. Before they spend a lot of money on bail, they might want to wait and see if charges get filed. A deadly weapon can be anything; it could be a golf club, it doesn't have to be a knife or a gun. Sometimes that weapon is found on a person; sometimes it's not. A lot of people immediately make bail, and shell out a substantial amount of money. If charges don't get filed, they don't get that bail money back.

The DA has 72 hours to file charges, if they don't, they'll be released. Before people start hiring lawyers and doing all this stuff I say, "Let's wait and see if charges get filed." In some cases, "Okay, I was arrested, I had a gun on me. Someone's been shot. There are 25 witnesses." Charges are definitely going to get filed in that instance. In that case, the first thing to do would be to figure out if you're going to hire a lawyer or go with a public defender and then figure out bail.

Tip from the Law Offices of Saul Bienenfeld, P.C.

Don't talk to anyone. Don't talk to the police. Don't talk to the district attorney. Don't talk to anyone, but your attorney and we'll do the talking for you. There is no one who works for the government who is your friend. As friendly as they appear and as nice as they speak to you, no matter how many sodas and donuts they buy you, they're not your friends. They're there for one purpose and that's to get a conviction. Have a professional speak to them at every stage of the game.

A lot of people think they can get out of charges by coming up with a strong self-defense, which may be possible, but if you share your self-defense with the police and they punch holes in it, you have ruined the entire self-defense case. Don't try to be smarter than the police or the district attorney. Have your attorneys make a statement.

There are a lot of clients who think that they're smarter than the police. They're going to make a statement. Most of the statements are videotaped. It's very hard to say that the police or a witness got it wrong when statements are videotaped or at least audiotaped. The only way to get around it, depending on how bad the statement is, is to try to have it suppressed on whatever violation of the Constitution there was, or to live with it, and to use it as part of your defense.

CHAPTER THREE

WHAT IF SOMEONE IS ARRESTED FOR DRIVING CRIMES?

Tip from Thomas Daly, Criminal Defense Attorney

If you ever get arrested, the number one thing is to stay quiet and ask for an attorney. The best advice you can ever get is to keep your mouth shut and get an attorney because anything you say can and will be used against you in a court of law. That really is true, especially in hit and run cases because they have to prove that you hit the car or property and did the damage. More often than not, most of the evidence they end up having against you is from your own statement. Really, it's extra important in that type of situation to stay quiet.

Other than that, a lot of these types of cases, depending on the severity, can often be settled out of court. Most times misdemeanor cases where they have a hit and run, I settle it out of court and get the case dismissed. The victim generally doesn't care too much. As long as they get paid for the damages, they're happy. That's why getting an attorney who knows what they're doing can help keep your rap sheet clean.

The worst case I've dealt with was a felony property damage charge where a couple of kids weren't using their heads. They were young, maybe in their twenties or so; they went and spun donuts at a school parking lot, out on a school field, and across the school grounds, ripped up a whole bunch of football turf, and then smashed into the fences a couple of times with their truck. The property damage was somewhere around a couple hundred thousand dollars.

The fines themselves weren't too bad. They were standard misdemeanor fines. The hefty financial burden there was fixing the damage.

That was a lucky case because we were able the get a lot of support from the community. The kids had been around the community for a number of years and were seen as good kids who made a stupid mistake.

I was able to play that angle hard and get the case reduced to a misdemeanor. A lot of it came down to them being willing to work to make up for the mistake they'd made. Plus, they were out there doing physical labor to help fix a lot of the damage, and that went a long way.

Tip from Phillip Moffit, Attorney at Law

Be polite to the officer. There's no need to argue. It's not going to help you one bit. Do not go around admitting that you knew you were doing something wrong. Just be polite and keep your mouth shut.

Do not try and talk your way out of it. Do not argue with that police officer. For any criminal charges, I would find an attorney that deals with that area and speak with them as soon as possible. Do not try to fight your attorney. Do not hide details from your attorney. Give them as much information as possible so that they can better help you.

We deal with a lot of people who don't tell us all the facts. It would be useful to know everything ahead of time because it helps us decide what's best for our client. Without knowing all the facts, I'm not going to know what's the best option.

A suspended license charge can get someone a ticket. They either get arrested, get out and call us, or they get the ticket, are told to show for the court date, then to give us a call. We get the court date and go on their behalf. The main thing for driving on a suspended charge is always fixing the problem. Whatever needs to be done to get their license back, we work on getting that done as quickly as possible. Even if it doesn't help this current case, we don't want them to have another case afterwards for the same thing. The consequences may be harsher the second time around.

When somebody calls me for a suspended license, I do what we need to do to get a license and then go over the facts. Firstly, I see why they got pulled over. If it looks like they got pulled over for a valid reason, it's most likely in their best interest to try to enter a plea with the court and work something out with their state so it doesn't count towards habitual traffic offender status. In Florida, as a habitual traffic offender, if you get three driving on suspended license charges in five years, your license will be suspended for five years. We try to avoid that. Sometimes that works by amending the citation to a different charge. A whole bunch of factors go into it, but for the most part, we work to get their license back and show the court that everything is better at this point.

Tip from Roger P. Foley, The Law Office of Roger P. Foley

First, I think the most important thing to note with DUI defense is that it's one of those areas of law that every Tom, Dick, and Harry lawyer attempts. However, it's an area that requires an enormous amount of knowledge. Fighting a DUI is hard work. The amount of work to properly defend a DUI is similar to that of a drug trafficking case. The attorney needs to know the applicable case law and be able to find the legal issues/mistakes in the case.

For instance, I am a member of the National College of DUI Defense, NCDD. They have a seminar at Harvard University every year. It's a week long. You are taught by the best of the best. There are additional seminars throughout the year, so you receive the case law updates and learn about the newest challenges. These additional classes take time, energy and financial resources. Being excellent takes effort, and only those with passion and discipline will take the initiative.

The NCDD has server boards where we work with each other. For instance, if I'm in the middle of a trial and need help, I can text in and get help from these hardcore guys that concentrate on DUI defense. Fellow members help on a minute's notice.

Another thing that I would recommend is to be wary of a lot of accolades on websites. Websites aren't the be all to end all. Be careful about this award and that award. Look them up. There are so many accolades out there that sound great, but mean nothing. Do a little research. I want a warrior as an attorney. I say this jokingly, but I believe that when you need a criminal defense attorney, or a DUI attorney, if it's not somebody that you would go to battle with, why would you hire them? If you don't think that person can help you in that type of situation, he probably can't help you in the courtroom.

If he doesn't have aggression in his tone when it's time to fight, then there is a problem. Obviously, there are times where you have to kiss and play nice, but there are more situations that call for a fighter. For instance, on a third or fourth DUI, at least where I am located, you're usually facing 18 months in a Florida state prison. If your attorney is kissing ass too much, you're probably going to be doing 18 months in custody. The prosecutors are going to love him and say he's a great guy, but as a defense attorney your goal is to help your client, not to be loved by everyone. You're going to battle, it's not about friendship. The client comes first.

The battle begins and it's about fourth amendment issues; it is about the fourteenth amendment issues. There are a lot of processes in a DUI, and that's why I started by stating that there are too many lawyers who say they do DUIs, but they don't. They are bottom feeders preying on those people who need help, and taking their money without doing the work. I would say that where I am in South Florida, between Dade County and Palm Beach County-that's three counties and I don't know how many millions of people-there are probably five, or six quality DUI attorneys. If I were arrested, obviously I wouldn't represent myself; there are five or six attorneys worth their fee. Lawyers that don't take the time to do the extra schooling, to take the courses, to find out the newest techniques, and the latest challenges are a waste of money. DUI attorneys need to know the case law and speak up for the client. They need to understand how to make a record for appeal. They do not need to clam up when a judge speaks aggressively with them.

Attorneys don't always do that, it's extra work and it can piss off prosecutors or judges. If they can charge someone the same price and plea them out, then the client suffers two-fold. On a third DUI, the client is facing incarceration. Most of the time you file a motion to suppress, which is dispositive, so if you win then the case is over. You're not pleading a 3rd or 4th DUI, so you really need to know that your lawyer is not just a plea lawyer. Ninety-seven percent of state cases are plea-bargained. Make sure that your attorney does not plead 100% of his cases. You've got to have an attorney that files motions to suppress, motions to dismiss, and who can go to trial and has been victorious, because if he's not, you're in trouble. No attorney can guarantee future results, but look for passion and look at past results. Ask any potential DUI attorney for his past 100 DUI results. Don't just accept the top five victories of his a career that he posted on his website.

The consumers don't know, and it's scary. The general public thinks that all lawyers are the same. There is a huge difference among attorneys, just like in other professions. I see things in court every day, scary things that get plead out. The state attorney's office has no duty to search for a mistake in a probable cause affidavit or to call the police officer out on it.

For instance, when I went into court today, I saw the prosecutor at arraignment, and he handed me the discovery. In the first two sentences of the Probable Cause Affidavit, PC, I knew that there was a fourth amendment search issue, and that the police seized my client without PC. The case shouldn't have even been filed. Meanwhile, the state attorney was offering me a guilty plea and an adjudication. Adjudication equals conviction. The conviction would cause my client's driver's license to be revoked. Additionally, a conviction cannot be sealed or expunged from the client's record.

It's not the prosecutor's job to find the mistakes made by police, so if your defense attorney doesn't search for these issues. you're in trouble. I pointed out the glaring error and the prosecutor told me to put something together and that he would consider dismissing it. Putting something together means research and writing and hours of work. Make sure your criminal attorney is willing to do what it takes to fight for you. An attorney that plays nice with everyone can help at times, but having an attorney that has gone to war with state attorney's office earns their respect. When a defense attorney is both liked and respected, the client receives these benefits.

Tip from Michael J. Palumbo, Palumbo & Associates P.C.

Don't talk about it with anybody, and you've got to reach out to a lawyer. Talk to no one.

Even if they already talked to someone, the same advice applies. Keep your big mouth shut. Get a lawyer immediately. You're in deep trouble. DWIs are no joke.

They're facing possible permanent loss of their driving privileges. Permanent revocation which, when that kicks in, they can forget it. They're not seeing a driver's license in any state. They're facing incarceration. They're facing a permanent criminal history.

If they get pulled over, don't say a word ever. Don't talk to the cops. Don't answer their questions. Don't do a field sobriety test. Don't do anything.

You're going to be arrested anyhow. The cops already know what they're going to do.

Tip from The Law Office of Edward J. Blum

Once a cop asks if you have been drinking, everything after is part of a DUI investigation to gather evidence to be used against you. At that point you don't have Miranda rights, but you can use your own common sense, you don't have to do what he's telling you to for the most part. For instance, he's going to ask, "Do you know why I stopped you?" Just say no. Don't give him any ammunition. If he asks if you have been drinking, say, "You know ... I've heard that I don't have to answer your questions and so I choose not to answer."

If you've been drinking, chances are he's going to pull you out of the car, and ask you to do field sobriety tests. Again say, "I understand that these are not mandatory, I don't have to do them, and so I choose not to do them." All those field sobriety tests are designed to fail so that the officer can gather information that will later be used against you in any criminal proceeding. The officer's then going to ask you if you want to take a preliminary alcohol screening test, and in California, at least, this is discretionary, you don't have to take it.

Check with local laws, but if you don't have to take it, don't, it can only hurt you. If you have alcohol on your breath, the machine is highly inaccurate, chances are you will wind up being above .08 and you'll get arrested. Once arrested, most states have what is called an implied consent law. This implied consent law says that you have to take either a breath test or a blood test. For California, you want to take the blood test, because there are ways to fight the blood test, more so than the breath test.

They're going to ask you questions, don't answer the questions. They're going to ask you to do a field sobriety test, don't do the field sobriety test. They're going to ask you to do a preliminary alcohol screening device test at the scene, don't do that. Once you've been arrested, you have to give them a test. You have to do a test, or you'll risk a refusal. A refusal results in a license suspension. If you refuse to take the chemical test after you've been arrested, it makes it nearly impossible for them to convict you of a DUI; but because the DMV are unscrupulous and don't really care, it makes it much more likely that you're going to have a license suspension in California for a year. Some states slightly less, but in all states it's more punitive than if you were to take that test post-arrest.

After you've been released, the first thing you need to do is get a lawyer, but also start the DMV hearing. Usually you only have 10 days after arrest to secure that hearing, and if you don't request it, then your license will be suspended in 30 days. If you do request it, you can keep your license for longer, and you can use the DMV proceedings as a method to gather discovery. The advantage is that they can make the cop show up at the DMV hearing where he doesn't have a prosecutor or anybody else there to protect him and he's usually not as prepared as he will be later when he speaks at the criminal case.

CHAPTER FOUR

WHAT IF SOMEONE IS ARRESTED FOR DOMESTIC VIOLENCE?

Tip from the Law Offices of Gerald E. Smith

The first thing is check that the evidence substantiates that accused committed the crime. In other words, does the victim have some bruises? If that is the case, where she does have bruises? If the evidence substantiates her version, you then would want to try to mitigate the possible sentence. Even if it is their second time being charged with a domestic violence charge, the accused will likely have to be enrolled in a Domestic Violence Recovery Program. In order to show the court that your client is taking the case seriously, have him enrolled in the program or an anger management course.

If the case also involves alcohol, it is advisable to get your client to attend Alcoholics Anonymous (AA) meetings and to document his attendance. Your client needs to mitigate the possible sentence and show the prosecutor that his actions may have been an aberrant behavior. The prosecutor will likely ask for some custody time if there are visible injuries. It is not uncommon for the prosecutor to ask for 60-120 days in custody, in addition to the 52-week Domestic Violence Recovery Program.

The defense attorney's job is to show the court that his client is taking the case seriously. If it is his second time being charged, look at the evidence and see if there is an underlying problem. Is alcohol involved? Drugs? Or maybe there is a psychological condition that is causing the outbursts. It is the defense attorney's job to help his client and not just plead him guilty. In regards to psychological issues, if you believe that this may be a problem, then you should get a psychological evaluation. The evaluation may reveal a condition that explains his actions and can now be treated. Again, your job is to help mitigate the sentence. Although the psychological issues may not be as common, there were a few cases that did require that we obtain a psychological evaluation and the results were helpful in getting the client treated as well as avoid significant custody time.

Finally, in a majority of the cases, the evidence will suggest that your client is an angry person who does not think twice about hitting a female (I use the male gender in the explanation, but the female gender likewise commits a significant number of the domestic violence cases). It may be that morality in our society has degenerated to that point that a person believes it is acceptable to slap or use force against a woman out of anger. I've heard this too many times, "She deserved it because she pissed me off." It is always someone else's fault.

As a defense attorney, it is our duty to help educate our clients on the law and to explain to our clients that society still does not find it acceptable to slap, hit or injure our spouse or significant other. Further, it is our job to fight for our clients if the evidence does not substantiate the charges. If that means you go to trial, then you go to win. There are a lot of defenses that can be used in assault/battery cases, but it is the defense attorney's obligation to review the discovery and determine if the case can be won, or whether it should be negotiated out.

Tip from Maureen F. Baldwin-Domes, Attorney At Law

First I would want to know the current status of the relationship? Is the couple still together? Is the couple separated? Most of the time, people accused of domestic violence are a boyfriend, girlfriend, same-sex partners, or married. If the relationship is over, I would certainly advise them not to talk to the other person, in the event the other would person were to make something up.

The problem is that these cases are completely different from each other. There's no blanket piece of advice other than if this person has been falsely accused by someone he doesn't know well, which would be to stay away from them. If someone has been accused of domestic violence by his girlfriend, or partner, generally the situation is one where they cannot trust that person anymore.

Most domestic violence cases are not like that. In many domestic violence cases those involved typically have an ongoing relationship, and there's a misunderstanding over a certain issue. I will generally tell my client not to alienate his spouse, or girlfriend, or boyfriend, or partner, or whatever, but not to discuss the case with them either.

Tip from Daniel Izquierdo, Criminal Defense Attorney in Miami, FL

The first tip is definitely under no circumstances to continue to, or attempt to, make contact with the alleged victim in that case. In Florida, when you're arrested for domestic violence, you immediately have to see a judge. At that bond hearing, the judge will put a "stay away" order in effect where the defendant can't have any contact with any of the victims in the case. Often people in domestic violence cases don't take that order as seriously as they should. They tend to think that everything is going to blow over, that the victim's okay and has forgiven them. Then, out of nowhere, the victim reports that he's been making contact with them and now the person is facing potential revocation of the bond and they're also going to add another charge for not obeying the court's order.

Definitely, the first tip is "Under no circumstances make contact with the alleged victim while the case is ongoing." The second one is "Make sure that you hire the best lawyer that you can and, most importantly, the one that you feel most comfortable with." That's how I define the best lawyer. Not by price, not by accolades, just make sure that they practice criminal defense regularly and they're the one that you feel most comfortable with. At the end of the day, if you hire somebody just because you could afford them, but you're not comfortable with them, what do you have?

CHAPTER FIVE

WHAT IF SOMEONE IS ARRESTED FOR DRUG CRIMES?

Tip from Tigran Martinian, Martinian & Associates, Inc.

A first time drug offender for meth use is not in a good place. The first thing I would do is see if the user has family members or some kind of support group behind them. It is very difficult to get off a drug by yourself, and most people do not succeed.

In Los Angeles, there is a government-sponsored program that first time offenders can attend. If they're willing to go there, get help, and not break the law for at least a year, they will be in good shape and not need more in the way of legal help.

I would also explain to them consequences of what is happening to them. Meth has such a powerful hold on their brain that it's hard for them to get off the drug. They have to understand the repercussions of what they're doing. The drug can destroy more than just the user's life. Entire families can be destroyed. People can lose their job, their dignity, spouse, their kids, their house, and more.

Now if I represented someone who was caught selling meth for the first time, I would first talk with them about the harm they are causing others.

Also, I would look for a way to suppress the evidence so that I could get them the best shot possible to lessen the degree of the crime.

Tip from Guiseppe Rosselli, Attorney at Law

The first piece of advice is that the system isn't about fairness. It's about making good decisions from this point forward based on the circumstances that you find yourself in. It's not about what actually happened, it's about what the police allege happened and how to make good decisions from this point forward to protect that individual's freedoms, and/or any other secondary consequences that may be associated with it.

Where they're at procedurally influences what can be done. It depends on if they were just arrested, or if they are scheduled for trial. The first thing they need to do is hire counsel, obviously. My position has been and will always be that that's the only decision, the only true decision that the defendant has, is who they want standing next to them at the time when they need to be presented in front of the court. That relationship requires trust on both ends (that my client will follow my advice that has been given and that I will follow through with what the defendant is trying to accomplish through the defense). If I'm not that person, then I don't want the case.

Whether someone is black or white, there's no difference in the advice that I give, but there's a huge difference in how they're being prosecuted.

For example, a young white kid with 10 stamp bags and $200 in his pocket, depending on that individual's prior record and interaction with police, may be someone who has the drugs for personal use. An African American in the same set of circumstances in a different neighborhood with a different set of cops, he's looked at as a drug dealer.

Although I know that racism is something that is very evident in our system, I don't believe that the primary racism that we see is that individual racism. I think it's more institutional. I think it's more subconscious, but nevertheless, it's as dangerous and as offensive.

Tip from Howard Greenberg, Attorney at Law

Never ever talk to the police. Keep your mouth shut. The only time it makes sense to talk to the police is if you kill somebody, and then give them a lengthy self-serving statement that will obviate the need for you to testify at a trial.

That will be your testimony in the worst crime that is memorialized in our books, the crime of murder. Let's return to drug crimes. The reason you never talk to the police is because the police lie. Their lies will poison everything they say, including the parts that are true. If they didn't lie in every one of these cases, we would not be able to defend our clients, but I have achieved monumental victories in cases that many other lawyers thought were impossible because the police lie for their team.

If the police simply told the truth, we would never be able to defend any of these cases.

CHAPTER SIX

WHAT IF SOMEONE IS ARRESTED FOR FRAUD?

Tip from Labe M. Richman, Attorney at Law

Insurance fraud cases are where you have enterprises that churn out insurance claims. They get people who are hurt or not, and they sign them up. Then they overcharge for different things like therapies, or for soft goods, like beds, and neck collars. They'll put down $200 for something that costs around $3.

These are set up like mills. They might do Medicare, they might do Medicaid or they might tackle your health insurance company. That's a huge crime in New York. The key issue in all of those cases is whether you knew that the claims you were submitting were fraudulent. Often these types of organizations have people at many different levels: they have a secretary; they have receptionists; they have a person who fills out the forms and makes the claims to the insurance company, etc. Usually those companies have a medical facility, or entity that is refers people to them, like people who are injured in car accidents.

One of the big things is that there is no fault insurance in New York, so you can't sue for under $50,000, unless there are serious physical injuries. Often the insurance covers that stuff. Car insurance covers the no fault claims. People have neck aches, headaches, and backaches, so they go to physical therapy. People churn up the bills.

The key issue is not making a statement because if you get picked up and you're the secretary or certain low level people, it's going to be very hard for them to prove that you knew that what you were doing was false. Higher ups may have said, "Okay, fill this out, put in this code, do it this way," and you, as an employee, may not know better. If you remain silent, they may have a hard time proving guilt.

In fact, you may be innocent. Let's say you go in, you talk to the government, and you say, "I didn't know." That doesn't really help because it's the same as if you say nothing. They have to presume you're innocent. If you say you didn't know, then they may write down the statement a little bit differently. You may give them information that will conflict with the facts. They may start asking you specific things. You may say the guy came in on Tuesday and they may have him coming in on a Friday. Then you look like you're hiding something. It's much better to say nothing.

That applies to any case. If law enforcement comes up to you and says something, say, "I want a lawyer," or just sit there and be mute. People get silence anxiety and they want to say something, but you don't have to. It's okay to ask a question like, "Who are you? Why are you here? What are you doing?" If you have a lawyer, give the officer your lawyer's name.

I work on a lot of passport and immigration fraud because work for a lot of immigrants. They may have applied for a passport under a fake birth certificate 20 years ago. After 9/11, they have facial recognition software, so they can scan and recognize residents as a security measure. Now you're doing everything right, but you didn't 20 years ago when you first came to the country. They may look at DMV records and see that there are two people with the same picture ID that have different names. They approach you and say, "are you the person in this picture?" If you say "yes," or "no," it may appear that you've lied to a federal agent. By affirming or denying your identity in the picture with your name, even if you haven't committed a crime within the past five years, you made a statement that is perceived as false by those authority figures. By saying "yes" or "no", you have committed a crime in their eyes. You see what I'm saying?

Not making a statement is critical in that circumstance. The other side of the coin is that sometimes making a statement can help you. If you decide that they really have you, then go in and cooperate. In federal cases, sometimes getting a lesser sentence is dependent upon going in and cooperating against the other people. You want to have a lawyer who can assist you in making that strategy decision.

Many times, the police will try to trick you. This is in any case. They'll say, " This is your time to tell us what your defense is," and that's not true. The police can't decide who cooperates. It's the U.S. Attorney or the D.A. They prosecute your case. The police have no authority to sign up a cooperator.

Ninety-nine percent of the time, you'll have another time to state your self-defense. You can come in with your attorney, you can get a proffer agreement where they can't use anything against you, except under certain exceptions, and you will have much more protection with the attorney. Now that might not be the case if it's like on *Law and Order* where there's a child dying in the trunk of a car and you can help them find that child now. If you wait to get a lawyer before talking about it, the child may die, and then your chance of cooperation will evaporate. Most of the cases allow you enough time to see your lawyer where you can weigh the options and choose the proper defense.

Typically, in cooperation deals you plead more, but you get less time because the judge is told how much help you gave. You actually plead guilty to more because they try to make it look like you didn't get a deal when you testify. Let's say you're an immigrant and you're trying to get a deal that will avoid deportation. It might be better not to cooperate because then you plead guilty to less. You work out a deal for one crime and you get a certain sentence. If they don't have a lot of evidence, you're probably in a good spot, but if you've already tried to cooperate with the cops, and given them all this information, you don't have many options.

If you don't have much money, and you hire a private attorney to represent you in a criminal case, in the end that attorney is not going to do that much for you. It's much better to go with the public defender. It's one thing if you have a lot of money and you can hire a private lawyer. They're probably going to give you more service if you hire a private attorney because the public defender's office is overstaffed. I see so many people who went to some attorney and gave them like

$2,500 or something for some big case and then they plead them out because they can't afford to fight the case. They're not getting paid that much money. Whereas if they had a public defender, there would be an investigator that would look into it, and give them better representation.

There's this myth going around that all public defenders are bad, but that's not right. Just like in any organization, there are good people and bad people. People should not assume that a private lawyer is better than a public defender. In particular, people who are stretching their budget to pay aren't going to get much more service from a private attorney.

Tip from Jeff Davis, NYC Criminal Defense Lawyer

Many times, fraud cases result in a proffer agreement. If they haven't made a statement with regards to any proffer, that creates a situation where a defense attorney has more leeway that can botch a negotiation with the district attorney.

I generally tell people not to make a statement to the police, or the district attorney and to allow the attorney to do their job. If there is ever a need for a statement, it's better to be in a controlled environment.

I have people opening their mouths all the time and they think that they're helping their situation. When I turn someone one in, if there is a situation where a detective is looking for someone, I will try to arrange a turn in at a specific time, probably early in the morning on a day where I know I'll get to get them through the arraignment process that same day.

By doing a controlled turn in, it looks better to an arraigning judge and I ensure that the police are not going to question why. That's why I tell people to get an attorney right away. When an officer calls and asks for you to come in, that's when I say to get a lawyer because there's likely going to be an arrest.

Tip from Gregg A. Pinto, Attorney at Law

My top tip for anyone who was just arrested is don't say a word. It's never in your interest. Actually, this is a little bit more specific to a fraud case or an identity theft case.

Those cases require a little more investigative work by the prosecutor and/or detectives before they make an arrest. Frequently, on a fraud case or a white-collar case, this is not something that some beat cop figured out in his head and then decided to go arrest the perpetrator.

Frequently, an investigation is done over the course of many days, weeks, or months where you have either a prosecutor, or a detective squad that is specifically looking at some sort of crime. They know a fraud occurred and now it's just unraveling it to figure out who is at fault. By the time they place their handcuffs on you, it's likely that they already have a strong case.

A lot of times if they're investigating you and you haven't been arrested, they have no time constraint other than statutes of limitation, and those are long enough that they're not worried about it. They can wait it out and make sure that they have their ducks in a row before they arrest you.

If you answer questions and if you're arrested for that type of crime, all you're doing is confirming what they already know. You're probably facing an uphill battle. You don't want to give them a confession on top of it. If you're going to have a hard time defending yourself in the first place, don't make it worse.

I was an assistant DA in a unit that did a lot of fraud and identity theft investigations. That was frequently a chief concern of ours. Are we working on a case where someone has been arrested already, or are we trying to build up enough evidence to make an arrest?

If it was the second variety where you were building up enough evidence to make an arrest, you really had time to make the case rock solid.

I can line up my witnesses to know exactly who I need to testify in the grand jury to secure an indictment. I can do all of that before the defendant is ever arrested so that when the arrest happens, everything is seamless. My advice to someone when they get arrested is to not make matters worse by talking.

CHAPTER SEVEN

WHAT IF SOMEONE IS ARRESTED FOR MURDER?

Tip from Mahmoud R. Rabah, Attorney at Law

The number one tip for someone charged with a very serious crime is that they don't entertain wishful thinking.

In my experience, wishful thinking is a mindset entertained by many people charged with a crime or accused of some wrongdoing. This is the idea that everything is going to be okay; it is a belief that there's going to be a silver lining and that bad luck will change to good. It also manifests itself as faith in the criminal justice system and law enforcement.

I'm very sorry to say that this type of thinking, this wishful thinking, is the most damaging mistake many people make when dealing with a criminal case. I can't tell you how many guys walk into a criminal case with this idea that everything will sort itself out at the outset only to find themselves sitting in jail months or years later.

The reason why wishful thinking is so dangerous is that they lose perspective on what is important and what should be done to prevent disaster. For example, when a person is contacted by the police that they are wanted for questioning, almost every experienced defense attorney will immediately caution a client to not say anything and exercise their right to remain silent. And yet, because of wishful thinking, many people walk right into the clutches of law enforcement and offer up statements that typically doom them in subsequent criminal prosecutions. Another way wishful thinking rears its ugly head is when individuals charged with serious crimes don't seek out the best and brightest representative to fight for them in court. I can't tell you how many people I've spoken to who hated their assigned attorney or public defender, or felt that the attorney they had was not doing enough on their case. Despite these feelings, they remained with these representatives right up until an inevitable conviction. When I ask why they never thought to hire an attorney or seek someone else to represent them, I hear responses such as: "I didn't think I would be convicted" or "there was so many problems with the case, I didn't think I'd lose" or "my family didn't hire an attorney because we thought it would work itself out." Clearly, these were fatal last words.

Surprisingly, I've found people wishfully thinking even in the face of homicide charges. Individuals accused of such wrongdoing thought, "hey, I'm innocent, I didn't do it." They walk into a police precinct and try to talk their way out of a bad situation, and then they get convicted. I'm sorry to say that prisons are full of people who thought like this and didn't do anything about it. I can't tell you how many guys I've dealt with on appeal that had amazing defenses, but squandered this potential because they didn't fight hard when they should have or didn't seek help when they needed it.

My biggest and best advice to anyone dealing with a serious case such as murder, manslaughter, or attempted murder, is to avoid wishful thinking. It is a very dangerous mentality.

In fact, this is advice I use with anybody dealing with a criminal case, big or small. Don't lose perspective. If it sounds serious, it is serious. It's going to stay serious. You have to go in swinging from the start.

Tip from Joseph Indusi, Attorney at Law

The number one thing I would advise, especially if they haven't gotten a lawyer involved yet, is to not speak to the police about the incident. A lawyer can advise them on whether speaking to the police is in their best interest. Often times, there isn't necessarily a whole lot of evidence. In hit and run cases, until the motorist, the person operating the vehicle, admits to being behind the wheel or admits to being intoxicated, evidence is sparse. Without such admissions, the police will not have the strongest possible case.

People talk too much and it is a natural human instinct to say something like, "Well let just me explain away what happened here. This was a misunderstanding." Just as a hypothetical, if you said something like, "I was at the strip club that night, but I didn't pull the trigger. I didn't shoot the guy," or something just as innocuous as that, it places you at the scene of the crime. If all the police had was surveillance footage of a guy who resembled your client, now he's admitting that he was actually there. The fact that they've got that statement, that the client was there corroborates with the suggestion that maybe the person on the video is your client, even if the footage is hazy. Something as simple as that could cause the person to be officially arrested.

Tips from Jeff Weiner, Former President of National Association of Criminal Defense Lawyers, based in Miami, FL (NACDL)

Tip 1 – Do not make any statement to the police, period. That means not in writing, not on videotape, and not when the police assure you that making a statement will help your case.

The person arrested should be polite and courteous. They should not resist in any way and should simply say, "I want an attorney." Period. That's tip #1.

Tip 2 – When the person is booked, they should not trust anyone in the jail, whether it's a corrections officer or a fellow inmate. They should not discuss the case with anyone other than their criminal defense attorney. That includes over the telephone with relatives, friends, or even a lawyer. Calls are almost always recorded.

Tip 3 – Get the best criminal defense attorney that you can afford. Do not call your family lawyer who does divorces or the lawyer that did the closing on your house. You need a specialist, preferably board certified in criminal law, with real experience, and a quality reputation.

CHAPTER EIGHT

WHAT IF SOMEONE IS ARRESTED FOR ROBBERY?

Tip from Shannon B. Schott, Esq.

The number one tip is to invoke your right to remain silent. Remember that you're always being recorded, regardless of who you speak to. There's always the chance that whatever you say is going to get back to law enforcement, so always invoke your right to remain silent.

Let's say an innocent person starts talking and their words get twisted. I'm in Duval County, Florida. If you are familiar with criminal justice, you know who Angela Corey is, and that this is a very tough place to be arrested. The law enforcement agencies here are top notch. The reason that we haven't had any race related incidents in the last couple of years is because all of our detectives, all of our law enforcement officers, must have a college education. You have intelligent law enforcement officers investigating your case who know all the tricks, and how to find the evidence.

If they can't find the evidence, they know how to manipulate the evidence to make someone look guilty, even when everything is circumstantial. The prosecutors are skilled at drawing inferences from circumstantial evidence. So even if you're innocent, you just need to stop talking because everything you say will be used against you whether you're guilty or innocent, in order to make a case.

Manipulation is very scary. That's why I do what I do. It's not because I care about what happens to one individual, it's because I think about what if that were me sitting there wrongly convicted or accused? Innocent people, maybe not angels, but people who are not guilty of the crime, are arrested and convicted every day.

Tip from David Storobin, Attorney at Law

Regardless of whether it's robbery or any other case, people tend to try to explain themselves, and they only make things worse by doing that.

Each and every time, they don't recognize the fact that what they're saying may be used against them. They think that it's going to justify things. The police are not there to make your life easier, it's not to help you, even though it may seem that they're being nice. Their job is to make sure that they get a conviction.

So, if you do get picked up, the first thing that you need to remember is to say that you want to call your lawyer.

Nine times out of ten, clients wind up saying something that's not helpful.

There's always a hearing that you can do that deliberates whether or not the confession was given voluntarily, whether the cops followed the procedure, or they violated that law. That hearing determines what's going to happen.

Having said that, at least in New York City, judges do not like throwing out confessions.

CHAPTER NINE

WHAT IF SOMEONE IS ARRESTED FOR SEX CRIMES?

Tip from The Law Offices of Robert Osuna, P.C.

The number one tip I would give a potential client who's looking for a lawyer is to get somebody who is well experienced in that area. You don't want an attorney cutting their teeth on a child sex abuse case because there's just a lot of particulars that go along with a child sex abuse case: a lot of expert testimony, a lot of medical records. Ideally, you'd want to get someone who's very well versed in that area. For example, most DWI's are going to be a misdemeanor. At the end of the day, the exposure is very low. Most child sex abuse cases, the exposure for prison is going to be very high. Twenty-five years in New York, up to life in prison depending on the circumstances.

I would suggest that someone gets a lawyer who's extremely well versed in child sex abuse cases. In murder cases, you'll need somebody who's well versed in dealing with experts because you have to deal a variety of doctors, psychiatrists, etc.

For someone just arrested, I would tell them to ask the lawyer how much experience he has with child sex abuse cases? Where he has defended them? Has he done them in the jurisdiction where the person was charged? Every jurisdiction is different. In New York City, every county has its own separate customs, even though it's all New York law. Get someone who's known in that jurisdiction, has a good reputation, and who has done that type of work before. If they don't know the right questions to ask, they're never going to get any answers.

In child sex abuse cases, there are certain things that unless you know how they work, the attorney wouldn't know to ask. Someone who's done extensive work in that field will ask the prosecutor who the outcry witness is. Where do they come from? Who's the expert you're going to use? What medical documentation is there? I would recommend a client always seek someone who has experience with those particular cases. There are a lot of criminal lawyers who have never worked on a child sex abuse case. They've never done a murder case. They've done a thousand DWI's and drug cases, but they've never done a child sex abuse. You want someone who knows to ask the right questions.

Tip from Erik B. Jensen, Attorney At Law

The best tip is to not make any statements to the police. The police may engage in some kind of deception in which they're trying to cajole the accused into making statements. Sometimes the police and the investigators will try to befriend them. Don't make a statement. You can never get in trouble for what you don't say.

A statement may not have hurt them, but if it did, the most obvious way is if they confessed to being at the scene of the crime, at the time of the crime. Or if they may have even confessed that they actually did it.

I had an uncle who raped three of his nieces over a period of about seven years. He was obviously guilty. Some of the people that I represent are actually innocent. Police can sometimes trip you up, upset you, or lead you into saying something that may make it sound like you're guilty.

My job is I never ask clients what happened. I always ask them, "What would the police say about what happened?" As a competent attorney and an officer of the court, you can't lie. You always have to be careful how you say things. In the interviewing process, you never get them to say what happened. You get them to say what the police would say happened. From there you can develop it.

My job is not to show that you're innocent. My job is to test the evidence in order to create reasonable doubt. In child sexual assault cases involving penetration, there are two things you look at: you look at the timeline and you look at the statements and facts. You just put it all together. You have to be really organized to do it.

Tip from Antonio G. Jimenez, Attorney at Law

The number one tip would be don't speak to the police. Most of the cases that we see, the suspect always talks to the police. They always try to explain the sex act or that the girl gave consent. It might be that a thirteen or fourteen year old girl did consent to it, but you can't legally give consent until you're eighteen years old.

A lot of sex crimes that we see have no physical evidence. There is no semen, there is no DNA, and there are no fingerprints. It's the word of the accuser, and then the client. The client will give their version of the events, which is usually a confession, and that hands down dooms their case. After that, they end up having to do a significant amount of prison time. Realistically, they could have gotten a much better offer without speaking, or perhaps even gotten their case completely thrown out, because then we attack the credibility of the witness.

If the witness is a teenager, then there's a very good chance that if it's a lie, we can get to the bottom of why she's making the allegation. Maybe it's against her stepfather because she was upset that he prevented her from going out, or because he's not her biological father and she developed a grudge. If he doesn't confess, then we have a good chance of discrediting the girl.

The number one tip, and the biggest tip, is to keep quiet. Don't say anything. Know that you're going to get arrested, and depending on the age of the alleged victim, you're either going to get a bond or you're not, but you're going to help your case by not speaking.

CHAPTER TEN

WHAT IF SOMEONE IS ARRESTED FOR THEFT?

Tip from Robert L.S. Angres, Esq.

As I tell all the clients, the best thing to do is remain silent, and exercise your rights. Those who don't talk usually walk. Not always, but usually.

When you're Mirandized, you are read your Miranda rights. You should always assert them because the police are trained to elicit incriminating responses from you. You're not going to be able to outfox them and even if you believe you're innocent, what will happen is if you tell them a story, you go to trial, and there are inconsistencies? Those inconsistencies will be brought out and used against you by the prosecution.

The less you speak, the better off you are because when you go to trial, if you go to trial, they won't be able to use inconsistent statements from you or twist words in such a way that you inadvertently incriminate yourself.

It's like a little law school professor told me. He said, "You know, Miranda rights help the smart criminals. The dumb guys can't help it. It just flows out of them like a river to the ocean." This sounds crude, but in the mafia movies, they always had a code of silence. The code of silence isn't there to entertain people, it's there to beat the crime or beat the prosecution. Silence is your best friend when faced with a criminal prosecution.

CHAPTER ELEVEN

WHAT IF SOMEONE IS ARRESTED FOR A VIOLENT CRIME?

Tip from S. Michael Musa, Criminal Defense Attorney New York

Get an experienced criminal lawyer immediately.

There are two categories of people who commit violent crimes: people that have no criminal background, or very little criminal backgrounds, typically those that are in the throes of passion or self-defense, or the other group of people that habitually commit violent crimes.

They must keep their wits about them, and get a lawyer. The first action from law enforcement is to get a confession, sometimes obtained fairly and sometimes obtained under false pretenses. False pretense situations are where someone, a detective or other investigator, may say, "we're only here to help you. We only want to know the truth. If you help us by telling us what happened, we will help you," which translates in the defendants mind to being, "I'm going to be released, I'm going home."

That is the number one trick used by law enforcement, and unfortunately upheld as a legal, valid strategy by the Supreme Court of the United States. In a case, maybe 20 years ago, Chief Justice Rehnquist, a Republican Reagan appointee, wrote the decision on that case, which allows the police to use trickery, subterfuge, and misrepresentations to obtain a confession.

So, you have a defendant that's being promised leniency or even freedom in exchange for the truth, when it's actually the exact opposite. When the defendant gives up his statement, his admission, or his confession, it is the cement that closes the coffin on his criminal case.

Tip from Kleon C. Andreadis, Attorney at Law

Let's roll that back one step. Someone who has been charged with a violent crime is going to be arrested, and, as we would say, put through the system; fingerprinted, rap sheet generated, go up before a judge for an arraignment, etc. Typically, in a violent crime, they're going to have bail set.

My number one advice to anybody who is arrested, irrespective of whether it is a DUI or a violent crime, is don't say anything. Be very polite. Tell them you'd like to speak to your lawyer, and call the lawyer. That's the probably number one tip: don't say anything until you've had a chance to speak to a lawyer, no matter what the police tell you.

People talk all the time and blow it. It's like trying to un-ring the bell. Probably very often people go ahead and make a statement. Why? Cops say, "It will make you feel better. Just write it down." "Okay." Or they've watched a little too much television. Remember *NYPD Blue*?

Many people don't fully comprehend what Miranda rights are. I had a client sit there, arms folded, legs crossed, just regaling the police with the story of how they robbed a house, and the people in it.

There was an international drug dealer that had just finished doing time in Brussels and got released. He had a choice of going to the Dominican Republic or to New York. He decided to come to New York. Tells his girlfriend, "Meet me there when I get out." He and a former partner of his, let's just say, had a dispute that ended up with the business partner being shot three times in the chest. My client gets off the plane. There are the detectives. The detectives know because Interpol tells them they're being released, so they're there waiting for them. My guy gets off the plane, says, "I knew you were going to be here. I thought you'd be looking for me."

He went with them, was a complete gentleman, and then started to tell the whole story of what happened. He said, "I feel a lot better that I've gotten this off my chest. You guys said if I cooperated, you'd take care of me, you'd be good, you'd let me go." He just admitted to killing somebody. Whether you have the defense of self-defense or not, even if you tell the police that it was self-defense, that's not for them to adjudicate. That's a defense at trial. He is now doing twenty-five to life.

When they make a statement, you have to go back and the district attorney has to serve you with a statement notice. At least that how it is here in the state of New York, and it's probably consistent in some of the other states. If a defendant made a statement that they intend to use at trial on their direct case, they need to serve you with a notice of that statement, and, as such, you're then entitled to what's called a Huntley hearing. To New Yorkers, a Huntley hearing is a hearing wherein you try to determine whether that statement was made voluntarily or not. If it wasn't, the judge will suppress it.

With homicide cases, at least in New York City, they videotape the statements, and sometimes you'll have a statement written in the defendant's handwriting. Other times, you'll have an oral statement.

If you're not free to leave, then you're deemed to be in custody, and if the police want to question you about the incident, they have to read you your Miranda rights. They have a sheet that they have you initial, and then sign off on each one of the rights. Invariably, when they get down to the last one, which asks if the signee would like to speak after their rights have been read, many say yes, and then go ahead and either give an oral statement, which the police write down, or they give a handwritten statement.

I've gotten statements suppressed over the years, but they're not often instances that you win.

Tip from Joshua Adams, Attorney at Law

For someone who was just arrested, I don't see how it's beneficial to cooperate with law enforcement. Especially in violent crimes, circumstances are different than in other crimes because you get a lot of crimes of passion. It is not necessarily people who are living a criminal lifestyle who end up getting charged with violent crimes. Moral people without extensive criminal histories end up getting arrested and charged with violent crimes fairly often.

Violent crimes are not typically planned. It's not part of some other crime. It's just something that happens. Maybe you're out drinking and you can't control your emotions, or maybe something unexpected happened. Because of that, I think that people who are charged with violent crimes, a lot of times they don't respond the same way as people who have a lot of experience in the criminal justice system. They want to make it better. They want to cooperate. They want to tell their side of the story. But in reality, there's not much of a benefit.

Generally, one of the first things you should do when charged with any crime is to invoke your right to a lawyer. Of course that's what a criminal defense attorney is going to say, but it's true. Invoke your right to a lawyer early and invoke it often. That's probably the number one tip. People involved in violent crimes that don't have a lot of experience with the criminal justice system think that things will be all right. I think it's a human nature thing, that when things are going bad, people have a natural, self-defense mechanism to think things are going to be okay. The criminal justice system will work itself out. Things won't be that bad.

The truth is, it's not always going to be okay. People go to prison. Families are torn apart. That's not necessarily a right away thing, but it is important to take things seriously enough to where you know you are putting resources into hiring a lawyer who's going to be able to spend time, who's going to be able to represent you, and put those resources into it because things are not always okay. You see it all the time. People who don't hire a lawyer even though they can afford one, they get a public defender, and then when things aren't going well, they want to hire a lawyer.

WHAT IF SOMEONE IS ARRESTED FOR A WHITE-COLLAR CRIME?

Tip from the Appellate Law Office of Stephen N. Preziosi

I'm located in Manhattan, New York. When someone is arrested on a Federal crime, the investigation is already done. The Federal authorities don't make an arrest until they've completed their investigation.

When State authorities make an arrest, they conduct the investigation afterwards.

This is a tremendous difference because I have to assume that if the Federal authorities have already made an arrest, that their investigation is complete. In white-collar crimes, this usually includes wiretaps, or some sour grapes. Somebody has cooperated and spoken with the Federal authorities extensively about whatever crime we're talking about.

In the Federal case, don't talk to the authorities. Hire a lawyer immediately. When you're dealing with the Federal Authorities, it's a crime to lie to them.

Let's say they complete their investigation and make an arrest, whoever is arrested will try to deflect or make themself appear innocent. If you're caught lying to the Federal Authorities, that is a separate and distinct crime.

The most important part of dealing with the Federal Authorities is that you never speak with them until you have a lawyer. Even if they can't prove the substantive crime that you're being accused of, if they can show that you lied to the Federal Authorities, they can prove that as a separate and distinct crime.

So, number one, don't talk to the police, and don't talk to the Federal Authorities, until you have a lawyer.

There are plenty who talk to the authorities when they shouldn't. It's almost like trying to unscramble an egg. Once your client has spoken to the authorities, whether it's Federal or State, especially in the Federal arena, you really need to be proactive.

First thing as an attorney, you have to take a look at the evidence. The Federal Authorities are usually meticulous about putting together evidence before they make an arrest.

If you're dealing with the FBI or the DEA, you want to do your discovery quickly. Usually this evidence has already been put before a Grand Jury and an indictment has been handed down, even before an arrest warrant is issued.

Take a look at it a good look at the evidence. Talk to your client and be frank. This is what they have. I think they have a good case. I think they have a bad case. You want to get a general assessment of what the case looks like. It might entail hiring investigators to go out and speak to witnesses. You want to make a thorough investigation. How good is the evidence? What does your client have to say?

Tip from Paul Neuharth Jr., APC

Don't make any statements without having a chance to review them beforehand with an attorney. The reasons for that are the officers, or whoever the investigator is, can attribute any number of statements to the individual that may have not been made. Or they will ask leading questions that are designed to elicit an incriminating answer without granting the accused an opportunity to explain.

For example, it would be, "Is this the first time that you've embezzled from your employer?" Either the answer is no, there's been multiple events, or yes, it is the first time, and it is an admission. A lot of time, the person asking the questions is going to ask for a specific yes or no answer. About 70% of the time, people make statements without an attorney present and it's really hard to un-ring that bell if they've made incriminatory statements that they were tricked into making.

Occasionally I can help a client who made a statement by showing that, in fact, the officer or investigator had a history of directing statements. Find something that would exonerate the person, prove that it was a false statement, and in some cases, actually encourage people to record their own interview. If they're going to do an interview without an attorney, or it's impromptu, I would have them use their iPhone or some other device to at least capture that question and answer session, however brief it may be. The officers aren't required to give Miranda admonitions when they're performing the investigations. A lot of people don't know that. They think they have to be given Miranda rights at every stage. Only after they've been arrested does that actually come into play.

Many people think the police are there, that they're investigating, that they're going to give Miranda rights, but they don't have to do it. That's not so much for white-collar. There are other offenses that are DNA specific. For white-collar, do not make any statements without having spoken to an attorney first. Sometimes the attorney will go with them and make a statement once that statement's been vetted completely. A lot of times, the officers won't make a statement or let them make a statement if they have an attorney present. That should be a red flag.

Tip from
Bijan Sebastian Parwaresch,
Former Prosecutor

I think the most important thing is that when you hire a federal lawyer for a federal case, which white-collar usually is, you need to get somebody from a big city, somebody who has experience handling these types of cases, especially the numerical value involved in the fraud or in the white-collar crimes. Usually it is some kind of theft or deceit, and they always boil down to the amount of loss, or more plainly, the monetary value of the criminality. Only lawyers who have experience with cases in the high numbers could do justice for the defense. So that's the first thing, hire a lawyer from a big city.

Choosing a lawyer is invaluable and a decision that has to be made early on in the representation. White-collar crimes, by nature, are crimes that get prosecuted with a lot of evidence. It's not like street crimes where a couple of rookie cops pull together a case that's going to get prosecuted. With federal cases, there's a lot of surveillance, there's lots of documents, there's a lot of evidence. Based on the abundance of evidence, it is in the interest of a defendant to work with the government, or to assist in certain avenues, of their case.

That's only possible within hours or days of the arrest, so it's a very important to get legal representation in a timely fashion.

Because these white-collar criminal cases are so rich in documentation, it's important to note that when an indictment is opened up or an arrest is made against an individual, the individual only sees a very narrow range of information that the government has against them. It's critical to look beyond what's in the charging documents, and delve into how the government got the evidence, what other evidence they could have, what other informants or individuals the government might already have talked to, and foresee how this case is going to progress from the government's point of view. After that, it will be easier to make a good decision on how to handle the case.

www.ingramcontent.com/pod-product-compliance
Lightning Source LLC
Chambersburg PA
CBHW060629210326
41520CB00010B/1538